Barrio Billionaire Publishing (USA)

For Jada Nash
- V. S.

For my little sister Wendy
-B. S.

In memory of

David Savage
Rodolfo "Corky" Gonzales
Ramon "Chunky" Sánchez

Forward
"Jada's Dance for Chicano Park"

Jada's Dance for Chicano Park is a children's book by Authoress Vera Sanchez. It is our call to history of one of our greatest self-determinant actions of the Chicano Movement as experienced through the eyes, soul and dance of La Chicanita, Jada. An eight-year-old girl, Jada is practicing for her stage debut as a Chicana folkloric dancer in the anniversary celebration of the recent takeover of a plot of barren land under the Coronado Bridge in Barrio Logan Heights, San Diego Califas.

Jada's dance, her ceremony alongside the brave residents of the barrio honors the organizing, the marching, the protest, the human blockade; and, the sweat of transformation of a piece of land into una Flor del Barrio. A flower cultivated through struggle for Nuestra Gente, not just in Barrio Logan Heights, but throughout Aztlan: Chicano Park La Tierra Mia.

Jada's vision of her "Nana," and her elder's soothing words and strong reassurance harkens to all our elders' and antepasados' wisdom that pushes us forward with profound lessons in faith, love, commitment to service to others. "It's your turn, mija". Yes, it is your turn, Vera Sanchez. It is your time. It is your burden of love to carry on the struggle for Justice, Equity and Peace your Uncles, Dad and Familia Sanchez so valiantly fought for: and to which they committed their lives.

Jada's Dance for Chicano Park is our call to history. It is our artistic call to our young that it is their time now. Time to create, manifest their righteous space in this world through their lessons of art, poetry, literature, dance, song, theatre, sweat, blood and tears. As my Father Rodolfo Corky Gonzales once wrote: "Life and Death are twins, so let's dance . . . "

Vera Sanchez, mil gracias for such a moving and emotional account of our heroes who courageously raise the Chicano Park flag every year in April. Mil gracias to all who participate in celebration and commemoration of an enduring tangible time in our collective history. A history that, through this beautiful community park, and now, your children's book, continues to gloriously etch our presence in, and thread our grito of liberation of, Aztlan.

Jada's Dance for Chicano Park calls out to all our youth across this country: "It's your turn . . ."

Que Viva La Raza!
Rudy Gonzales
Denver, CO

Jada was practicing in her bedroom
before her performance,
even though she wanted to play outside.
But today, she had to get ready for
the Chicano Park celebration.

She repeated her footsteps.
1-2-3.
1-2-3.
Heel, stomp, flat.
Heel, stomp, flat.

Mommy peeked through the door,
watching Jada practice.

Children laughed outside her window,
as they ran through the sprinklers,
but the noise didn't break her concentration.

Mommy held a box wrapped in ribbon.

"Mija, there was a time we fought for this day.
Some people didn't want us to celebrate our park.
You must listen before you open your present."
"I promise," Jada said.

She closed her eyes,

imagining when the park was built.

Protesters waved their picket signs in the air.
Jada marched with them and chanted,
"This is our land! You will not take it from us!"

Jada's words soon turned into song lyrics.
She stood next to a large man with a handlebar mustache.
The large man played a wooden guitar, and she sang with him.

Jada grabbed a handful of seeds and planted them in the dirt.

She approached a group of women holding brushes and buckets.

Jada painted a rainbow with hearts on a pillar.

An angry man driving a bulldozer honked,
shouting for everyone to move out of his way.
He wanted to destroy all the hard work
people put into building the park.
Jada blocked the bulldozer to protect her rainbow.
"Leave now!" she commanded.

Jada locked her hands with
the protesters to stop the angry man.

Vera Sanchez is the
author of two novels. She has performed
for Chicano Park Day at the age of five
and was part of the mural restoration
project. Vera teaches college English and
creative writing. She grew up in Barrio
Logan and lives in San Diego.

Beto Soto is an artist who
has been inspired by Chicano Park.
He grew up learning about the artists
who have made the park look so
beautiful. Beto has been living in San
Diego since he was 12 years old and is
currently painting and drawing in the
city that he calls home.

CPSIA information can be obtained
at www.ICGtesting.com
Printed in the USA
BVHW021502020920
587600BV00006BA/96